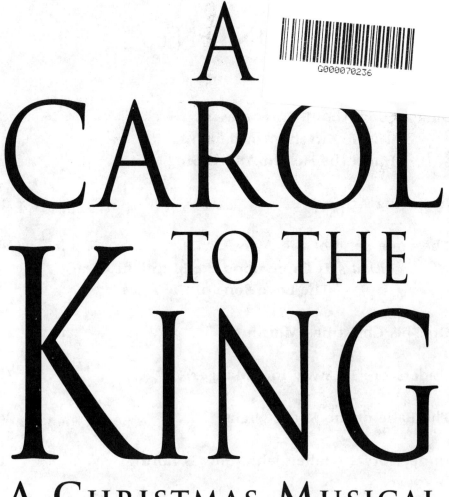

A CAROL TO THE KING

A CHRISTMAS MUSICAL

Written and Arranged by
MOSIE LISTER

Orchestrated by Steve Mauldin

LILLENAS
PUBLISHING COMPANY

lillenas.com

CONTENTS

Sing a Song About Christmas 3
  with Joy to the World *and*
  Hark! the Herald Angels Sing

In Loving Arms. 10

The Love Song of the Ages. 14
  Includes: It Came upon the Midnight Clear –
  The Love Song of the Ages

On This Christmas Morning 20

Underscore 1 (Away in a Manger). 25

The Babe of the Silent Night. 26

Underscore 2 (Hallelujah! Jesus Is Lord!) 30

Glorious Is the Lord Almighty. 32

Lift Him Up *with* Hallelujah! Jesus Is Lord! 38

Clip Art. 47

Sing a Song About Christmas

with
Joy to the World
Hark! the Herald Angels Sing

Words and Music by
MOSIE LISTER
Arranged by Mosie Lister

With majesty ♩ = ca. 92

CD: 1

Choir unison

Come on and sing a song a-bout Christ-mas,

4

Sing a-bout the Ho - ly Child, come down from a - bove.

Tell a-bout the joy with - in you, Tell a-bout the hap - py song.

Come on re - joice, lift your voice and sing,

CD: 3

sing a - long.

*"Joy to the World"
Two part choir

Joy to the world! the Lord is come; Let earth re - ceive her

6

*"Hark! the Herald Angels Sing"

Faster ♩ = ca. 110
Choir unison

CD: 5

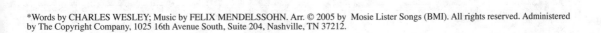

G D7 Am7 D7
Sing a song_ a-bout peace. Re - joice on Christ-mas morn-ing, let
Am7 D7 Gm 84 C B7 Em
hap - pi - ness in-crease. Join with those a - round you,
B7 Em C B7 Em A7
Sing a hap - py song._ Come on re - joice,_ lift your voice_ and
S.A.T.B.
G/D 88 D7
sing. Come on and sing a -
sing, come on and sing_ a -
G C G
long, sing a-long,_ sing a - long.
long.

Voice 1: (*without music*) The Word became flesh (*music begins*) and lived for a while among us. We have seen His glory, the glory of the One and Only, who came from the Father, full of grace and truth. *(John 1:14)*

Voice 2: The song started over 2,000 years ago, and it's still echoing around the world today. In every corner of the globe, you may hear the joyful melody sung by those who have seen His glory, those who have found God's promised Messiah for themselves!

In Loving Arms

Words and Music by
MOSIE LISTER
Arranged by Mosie Lister

The Love Song of the Ages

Words and Music by
MOSIE LISTER
Arranged by Mosie Lister

**Voice 1: "There were shepherds living out in the fields nearby, keeping watch over their flocks at night. An angel of the Lord appeared to them, and the glory of the Lord shone around them, and they were terrified. But the angel said to them, 'Do not be afraid. I bring you good news of great joy that will be for all the people. Today in the town of David, a Savior has been born to you; He is Christ, the Lord.'" *(Luke 2:8-11)*

Voice 2: "Suddenly a great company of the heavenly host appeared with the angel, praising God and saying, 'Glory to God in the highest, and on earth peace to men on whom his favor rests.'" *(Luke 2:13-14)*

The promised Messiah came into the world as an infant– tiny... helpless... weak. But He had within Himself all those things that God was– unlimited power, inexpressible glory, and overcoming love, a love that would change the world– a world that would change us.

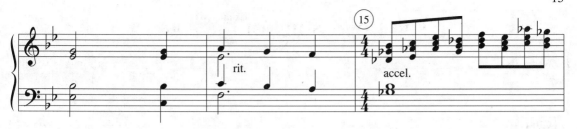

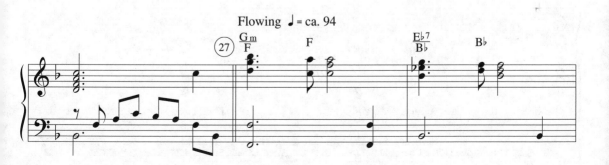

voic - es lift - ed high, 'Til peo - ple ev - 'ry -

CD: 15

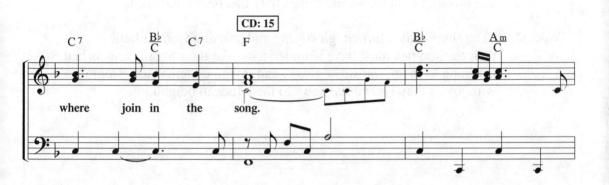

where join in the song.

D.S. al Coda
(to pg. 17, meas.48)

CODA

S.A.T.B.

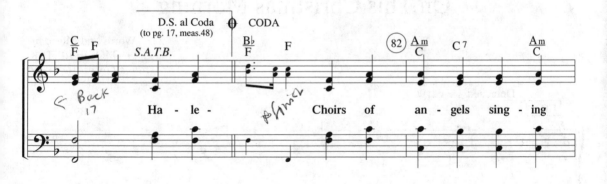

Ha - le - Choirs of an - gels sing - ing

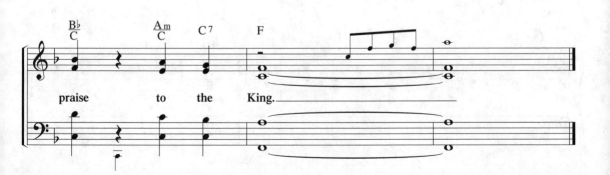

praise to the King.

Voice 1: "When the angels had left them and gone into heaven, the shepherds said to one another, 'Let's go to Bethlehem and see this thing that has happened, which the Lord has told us about.' So they hurried off and found Mary and Joseph and the baby, who was lying in the manger. When they had seen him, they spread the word concerning what had been told them about this child, and all who heard it were amazed at what the shepherds said to them. The shepherds returned, glorifying and praising God for all the things they had heard and seen."

Voice 2: "The shepherds returned, glorifying and praising God," I believe their testimonies must have sounded a lot like the song the angels had just sung to them. (*music begins*) I can imagine their voices singing with joy as they spread the news to their Judean neighbors.

On This Christmas Morning

Words and Music by
MOSIE LISTER
Arranged by Mosie Lister

Choir unison

⑨ E♭ *mf*   B♭7

1.Christ the Lord is born to - day,   Born in a man - ger,
2.Come on broth - ers, come and see.   Tell me__ how can

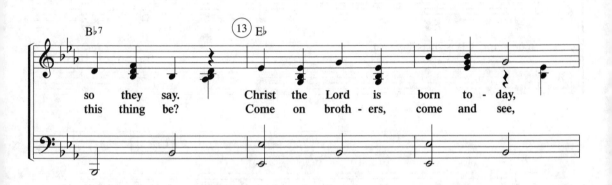

B♭7   ⑬ E♭

so they say.   Christ the Lord is born to - day,
this thing be?   Come on broth - ers, come and see,

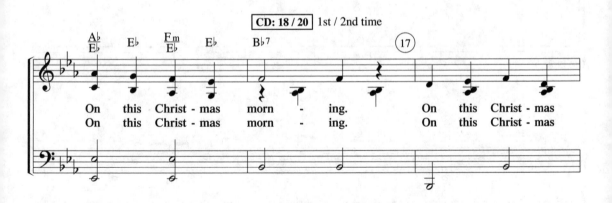

CD: 18 / 20 1st / 2nd time

A♭/E♭   E♭   F m/E♭   E♭   B♭7   ⑰

On this Christ - mas morn - ing.   On this Christ - mas
On this Christ - mas morn - ing.   On this Christ - mas

E♭   *S.A.T.B.*   ⑳ A♭   E♭/G

day.   Sing we now,
day.

Underscore 1

(Away in a Manger)

JAMES R. MURRAY
Arranged by Mosie Lister

Voice 1: " ' I am the Lord's servant', Mary answered. 'May it be to me as you
have said.' Then the angel left her...And Mary said, 'My soul glorifies
the Lord and my spirit rejoices in God my Savior, for he has been
mindful of the humble state of his servant. From now on all generations
will call me blessed, for the Mighty One has done great things for me–
holy is His name. His mercy extends to those who fear him, from
generation to generation." *(Luke 1: 38, 46-50)*

Voice 2: The song began before Jesus was born. Shortly after God's miracle had
begun to grow inside of her, Mary praised God with the beautiful song
that she sang. She knew that God had called her to be the mother of His
Son, and she trusted Him completely in all things, knowing that she
would soon bring the Holy One into the world.

And when the time had fully come, the shepherds hurried in from the
fields to see him! They shared the angels' song with everyone they met,
including Mary and Joseph, "And Mary treasured all these things and
pondered them in her heart." *(Luke 2:19)*

Segue to "The Babe of the Silent Night"

The Babe of the Silent Night

Words and Music by
MOSIE LISTER
Arranged by Mosie Lister
and Barbara Williams

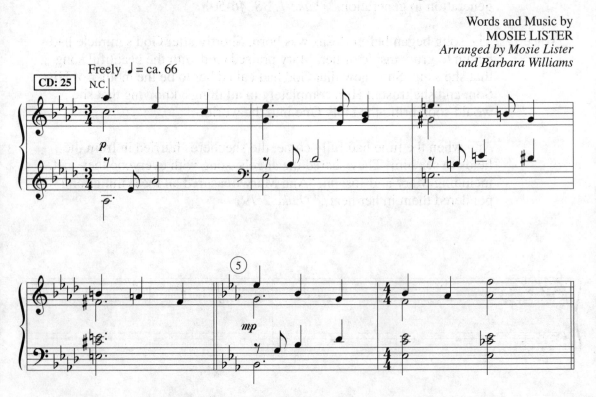

28

Voice 1: "For unto us *(music begins)* a child is born, to us a Son is given, and the government will be on his shoulders. And he will be called Wonderful Counselor, Mighty God, Everlasting Father, Prince of Peace. Of the increase of his government and peace there will be no end." *(Isaiah 9:6-7)*

Voice 2: And the song goes on, throughout all the ages. It began before His birth. It was sung by the angels to a handful of lowly shepherds on a lonely hillside, and now thousands upon thousands of us who know Him shout His name! We shout His name in praise and lift Him up. And the praise will go on and on....until His kingdom has fully come and we join the saints of all the ages in praising the Lamb. And then, forever with them in glory our song will blend with the song of the angels in endless praise and glory to our God.

Underscore 2

(Hallelujah! Jesus Is Lord!)

MOSIE LISTER
and BARBARA WILLIAMS
Arranged by Mosie Lister

Glorious Is the Lord Almighty

Words and Music by
MOSIE LISTER
Arranged by Mosie Lister
and David Miller Williams

Lift Him Up

with

Hallelujah! Jesus Is Lord!

Words and Music by
MOSIE LISTER
Arranged by Mosie Lister

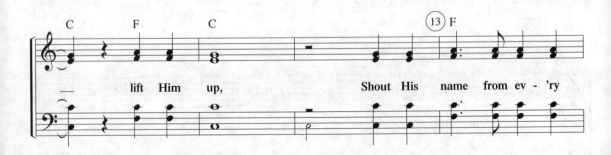

44

A CAROL TO THE KING

A CHRISTMAS MUSICAL

A CAROL TO THE KING

A CHRISTMAS MUSICAL

A CAROL TO THE KING

A CHRISTMAS MUSICAL

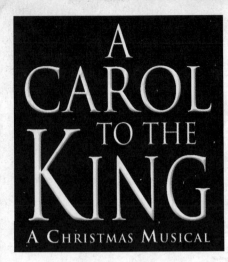

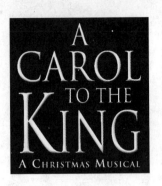

A CAROL TO THE KING

A CHRISTMAS MUSICAL